DISCOVER ● SCIENCE
COLD

Kim Taylor

Chrysalis Education

DISCOVER SCIENCE

Contents

US Publication copyright © 2003 Chrysalis Education
International copyright reserved in all countries.
No part of this book may be reproduced in any form
without written permission from the publisher.

Distributed in the United States by
Smart Apple Media
1980 Lookout Drive
North Mankato, Minnesota 56003

Copyright © Chrysalis Books PLC
Text © Kim Taylor Times Four Publishing Ltd
Photographs © Kim Taylor and Jane Burton
(except where credited elsewhere)

ISBN 1-93233-373-9
Library of Congress Control Number 2003102581

Designed by Tony Potter, Times Four Publishing Ltd
Illustrated by Peter Bull

Science adviser: Richard Oels, Warden Park School,
Cuckfield, Sussex

Typeset by Amber Graphics, Burgess Hill

Printed in Hong Kong

About this book

What really happens to water when it freezes? Which is the coldest part of the Earth? Why do insects move more slowly in cold water? And what *is* coldness, anyway?

In this book you can find out the answers to these fascinating questions, and many others. You can read about glaciers and icebergs, snow, and frost. Discover what damage cold can do, and how plants and animals survive cold weather. Learn, too, how people today create coldness and use it in many ways—for example, to preserve food, cool down hot places, and provide opportunities for fun and sport.

What is cold?

Cold is the absence of heat, which is a kind of **energy**. Cold things do not contain as much of that energy as hot things. If you put something hot against something cold, heat always flows from the hot thing to the cold. Some parts of the Earth's surface are naturally cold because they receive fewer of the sun's hot rays. We can also make things cold with machines, such as refrigerators and freezers. The coldest temperature possible is called **absolute zero**. This is minus 460°F (minus 274°C).

Brr!

It is difficult for humans to live in cold places because they have to keep their bodies warm. This man's mustache and beard became frosted while he slept.

Icebergs

The Arctic and Antarctic are very cold. Rivers of ice, called glaciers, form there. Pieces of glacier break off when they reach the sea and form icebergs.

Icebergs float on the sea. Big ones may last for months, drifting hundreds of miles before they finally melt in warmer waters.

Snow shake

Polar bears are protected from the Arctic cold by thick fur covering a layer of body fat. This bear is shaking the snow from its coat.

Heat energy

Everything is made of tiny particles that are too small to see. When something is hot, these particles are full of energy and vibrate a great deal. When it is cold, they **vibrate** much less. Nowhere on Earth is completely cold. Even the ice particles at the South Pole vibrate a little.

1   2   3

Water is made of tiny particles called molecules. This drawing shows what happens to water molecules at different temperatures. The molecules in the steam (1) are hot, so they vibrate a great deal and move in every direction. The molecules of liquid water (2) are cooler and move about less. The molecules in the ice (3) are cold because they have had much of their heat removed. They are held close together and cannot vibrate much.

Four leaves fell on this icy pond. Three blew away, leaving outlines in the air.

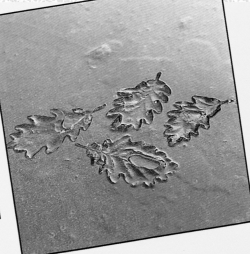

Now the fourth leaf has gone. Why have the leaves left "prints" in the ice?

Icy leaves

The sun's heat bounces off the shiny ice, but the fallen leaf absorbs the heat. As the leaf warms up, it melts the ice round it, leaving its exact shape behind when it blows away.

Cooling

Hot things lose their heat and cool down. For example, a hot potato in a cold room will eventually reach the same temperature as the room. Some of the potato's heat **radiates** away and is absorbed by the walls of the room. Some passes by **conduction** into the table on which it sits. Some passes into the air, causing **convection** currents that rise and carry the heat up and away.

Warm animals, such as this badger, radiate heat into the air. Another way this badge is losing heat is by **evaporation**. As the water on its fur evaporates into the air, it takes heat from its body and helps the animal to cool down.

Very hot steam is used to drive generators to make electricity. The steam is then cooled in huge cooling towers like these. Inside the towers the steam cools, condenses on the walls and drips down as water. This is then pumped away and turned back into steam again.

Sunset

Sunrise

After a day of sunshine, the surface of the Earth is warm. At night, this heat radiates back into space. Radiant heat travels at the speed of light, and the Earth's surface cools down very quickly.

Clouds in the sky act like a blanket and prevent heat escaping so fast. On clear nights, however, there is nothing to stop heat leaving the Earth. That is why clear nights are often cold.

Cold experiment

COOL IT!

You need
• A half-full glass of water
• A room thermometer
• A paper towel
• A thin rubber band

1 Leave the glass to stand for some hours until the water is at room temperature (check it with the thermometer).

2 Dry the thermometer. Then wrap a piece of paper towel (about 1in. square) around the bulb. Fasten it with the rubber band.

3 After a few minutes, read the thermometer and write down the temperature.

A duck can stand on ice and not suffer from the cold. Its feet are nearly as cold as the ice, so the duck does not lose much heat through them. The muscles that work its feet are in its legs and so are wrapped warmly in feathers.

4 Dip the thermometer in the glass of water so the towel is wet. Without touching the bulb end, wave the thermometer in the air for about 30 seconds.

5 Now read the temperature on the thermometer. Has it changed?

As water evaporates from the paper, it cools the thermometer down.

Freezing

When a liquid becomes cold enough to **freeze**, it turns into a solid. For example, at 32°F water turns into ice. As a liquid is cooled to its freezing point, **crystals** begin to form in it. Ice crystals are made of neatly arranged layers of water molecules (see the drawing on page 5). If water is cooled quickly, only tiny crystals form. Slow freezing produces long, dagger-shaped crystals.

Icicles

Icicles form when water drips in air that is colder than 32°F. Each drop leaves a thin layer of ice before it falls, and so the icicle grows. Water trickling over this branch has left icicles hanging off each twig.

Metal crystals

Metals melt when they are heated. As they cool down, crystals form and the metal freezes (turns solid) again. The crystals are packed tightly together. You cannot see them when you cut the metal open—but if you bend it until it breaks, the crystals show up clearly. These aluminum bars have been sawn part way and then broken. You can see the chunky crystals in the broken part.

This stream is covered in "cat ice" – that is, a layer of ice with air underneath. This makes it weak and only just able to hold the weight of a cat. You can clearly see the crystals in it.

Frost crystals on this window pane have made beautiful, feathery patterns like the fronds of a fern.

Even quite thick ice can be dangerous when the sun comes up and begins to melt it. This dog is in danger of falling through.

Cold experiment

THE EFFECTS OF SALT

Salt lowers the freezing point of water. That is why the sea is slower to freeze than freshwater, and why salt is put on roads to clear them of ice in water. Test this for yourself.

You need
- Two same-size plastic pots
- Water
- Salt
- A teaspoon
- Freezer or refrigerator

1 Fill both plastic pots three-quarters full of water.

2 Stir a teaspoonful of salt into one pot of water.

3 Put both pots in a freezer or ice-making compartment of a refrigerator.

4 Check at 5–10 minute intervals. How long does each pot take to freeze?

Did you know?

If a solid rubber ball is frozen in liquid oxygen to minus 321°F, it will shatter into fragments when dropped onto a hard surface.

Ice

Ice is frozen water. It occurs naturally in cold places, or it can be made artificially.

As it freezes, water expands. That is why house pipes sometimes burst in very cold weather. The frozen water in the pipes expands, breaking the pipe. It is also why ice cubes come out of the fridge deeper than the water you pour into the ice cube tray.

Climbing a glacier

This climber has spikes on his boots to help him climb a glacier. The weight of the ice in a glacier causes huge pressures that melt it a little, so the glacier moves a few inches each day.

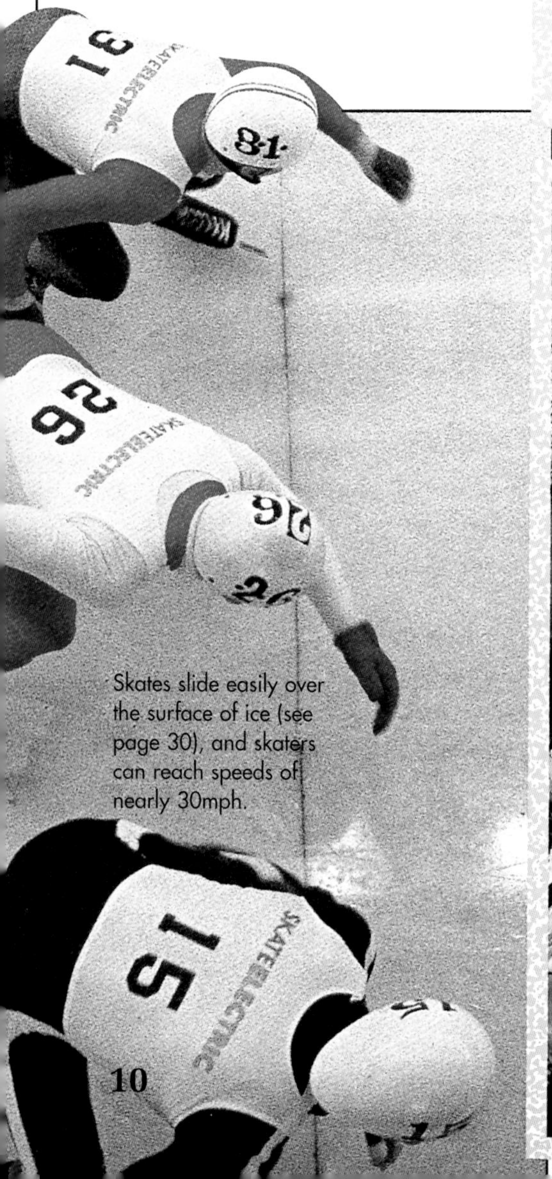

Skates slide easily over the surface of ice (see page 30), and skaters can reach speeds of nearly 30mph.

The small picture shows a thin sheet of ice with two leaves and lots of bubbles in it. The big pictures shows the same ice viewed through two pairs of polarizing glasses held at right angles to each other. The crystals in sheet ice can only be seen when it is viewed in polarized light.

Sky ice

High clouds are made of tiny ice crystals that can act like **prisms** and split the light into colored patterns.

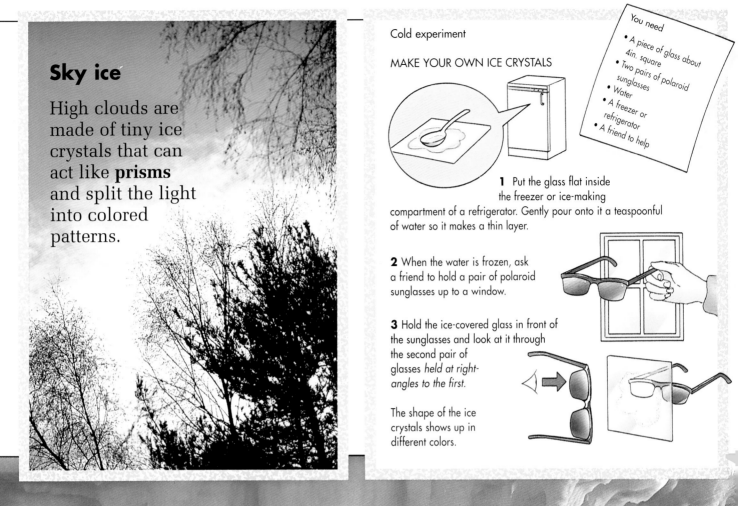

Cold experiment

MAKE YOUR OWN ICE CRYSTALS

1 Put the glass flat inside the freezer or ice-making compartment of a refrigerator. Gently pour onto it a teaspoonful of water so it makes a thin layer.

2 When the water is frozen, ask a friend to hold a pair of polaroid sunglasses up to a window.

3 Hold the ice-covered glass in front of the sunglasses and look at it through the second pair of glasses *held at right-angles to the first.*

The shape of the ice crystals shows up in different colors.

Floating ice

Icebergs, like ice cubes, float because ice is slightly less **dense** than water. This iceberg is gradually melting. During stormy weather, huge waves crashed against it, carving it into beautiful shapes.

Did you know?

Before refrigerators were invented, people used to gather ice in winter and store it in caves. The caves were lined with straw to keep heat from reaching the ice.

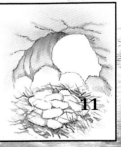

11

Frost

On a cold winter night, a thick layer of white frost sometimes covers everything from the grass on the ground to the roof tops. Frost is made of tiny ice crystals. They are not frozen water drops but form directly from **water vapor** in the air. The molecules of water in the air stick onto any ice crystals as soon as they start to form, making the frost crystals grow.

Frost crystals sometimes grow into fan shapes like these. Each piece of the fan is made up of many tiny six-sided crystals. You can just see some six-sided shapes at the tips of these fans.

Did you know?

Frost is less likely to form on the ground on a cloudy night. This is because the clouds hold in the heat given off by the Earth and keep the ground warmer.

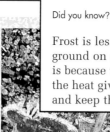

Frost often forms at ground level and not higher up. This is because there is more water vapor in air close to the ground. Here you can see long frost crystals sprouting like flowers from a piece of dead bracken lying on damp sand. Water has evaporated from the sand and formed crystals on the bracken.

Cold experiment

MAKE FROST FERNS

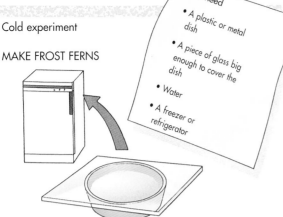

1 Pour enough warm water into the dish to cover the base. Cover the dish with the glass and put it in the freezer or ice-making compartment of a refrigerator.

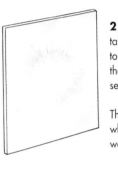

2 Wait several hours, then take out the glass and hold it up to the light. You should be able to see frost ferns on the glass.

The frost ferns were formed when water vapor from the warm water froze on the glass.

Quick freeze

When the temperature drops quickly, water molecules in the air freeze and form small frost crystals on every cold surface.

Slow freeze

When the temperature drops slowly, water molecules drift around and form big crystals like those on this leaf.

Frosty bear

Polar air is often very dry, so there is not much water vapor in it to form frost. However, this polar bear's warm breath contains water vapor that forms frost around its mouth and nose.

Snow

Instead of forming like frost on the ground, snow begins as ice crystals in a cloud high in the air. Each snow crystal is a tiny six-sided shape that floats down slowly. The crystals join together to form snowflakes. The snowflakes join together to form bigger flakes. A big snowflake may contain thousands of crystals.

If you look up into the sky when it is snowing, you can see the flakes coming down. They look dark against the pale sky, like a huge swarm of insects. The flakes drift in the air or rush along with the wind until they come to rest on the ground. If the ground is cold enough, the flakes will settle, building up into snow. The sun's heat is too weak to melt them.

Snow fun

You can travel quickly over ice and snow, if you have something smooth to slide on.

Snowy weather is a hard time for animals. The snow covers the ground and makes it difficult for them to find food. This squirrel is lucky, for it has found some fallen apples.

When the air is around 32°F, snow is wet and sticky. It sticks to trees and is so heavy that it may bend or even break the branches.

Cold experiment

MAKE A MODEL SNOWFLAKE

You need
• A piece of paper
• Scissors
• Pencil
• A pair of compasses

1 Set the pencil and the compass point 2in. apart. Draw a circle on the paper.

2 Put the point of the compasses on the circumference (edge) of the circle. Draw arc 1 (see the drawing above). Move the point to arc 1 and make arc 2 the same way. Repeat this until you have six arcs on the circle. Draw a line from each arc to the center of the circle. Cut out the circle. Fold it in half from arc 1 to arc 4.

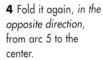

3 Fold it again from arc 3 to the center.

4 Fold it again, *in the opposite direction*, from arc 5 to the center.

5 Draw a snowflake outline as shown. Cut out the shaded parts. Open it up.

Animals leave tracks in fresh snow. Each kind of animal leaves its own pattern, and you may have to be an expert to identify them. This track was found in Greenland. It was probably made by a small Arctic animal called a lemming.

No man

If the weather is too cold, snow will not stick together. When snow is close to 32°F, the pressure of your hands can melt it a little so you can form snowballs and snowmen.

Did you know?

Snow is a light and fluffy form of water. If you melted a 2.5ft-deep layer of new powdery snow, it might contain only about a 0.75in-deep layer of water.

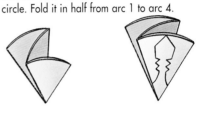

Plants in the cold

Plants have various ways of surviving the cold. **Annual** plants avoid winter by dying in the fall. They leave behind them only their seeds, which will grow in the spring. Many **perennial** plants lose the parts above ground in winter, but keep an underground food store to grow from in spring. However, some specially tough plants can stay above ground in extreme cold without damage.

This early flowering plant, the winter aconite, is a relative of the buttercup. It grows from a food store called a corm (see page 17).

Spring flowers

Some plants, like this snowdrop and the winter aconite (above), flower early, when snow may still be on the ground. Snowdrops grow from underground food stores called bulbs.

Snowdrops are woodland plants. They flower early so they can get some sunshine before the leaves of the trees open.

Cold experiment

GROW AN ONION

What happens to the onion as it uses up its food supply?

You need
- An onion
- A jar
- Water

1 Choose an onion that is larger than the top of the jar. Fill the jar with water and put the onion on top so that its root end is in the water.

2 As the days go by, watch the onion sprouting. It does this by turning the food store inside it into green leaves.

Spring bulbs, such as hyacinths, can be grown in the same way. They will produce flowers without needing any soil.

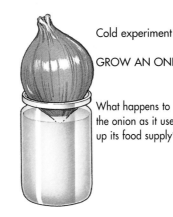

Food stores

Bulbs, **corms,** and **rhizomes** are all types of plants' underground food stores. Bulbs are swollen leaf bases. Corms and rhizomes are swollen stems. The crocus (left) grows from a corm. The iris (right) grows from a rhizome. You can see the rich pink plant food where the iris stem has been cut open.

Trees with soft leaves lose them in winter. The sap drains into the roots, so frost cannot harm the tree. Evergreen trees have tough, hard leaves so snow does not harm them.

Animals in the cold

Animals have to find ways of coping with cold weather. Some, such as the penguin, have bodies suited to life in the cold. Others cannot survive low temperatures and so they **migrate** (move to a warmer place) until the worst weather is over. Some large mammals, many birds, and even some insects do this. Another way some animals survive is to find a place to hide where they can sleep throughout the winter. This is called **hibernating**.

Food is scarce for many animals in winter. This hawk is lucky to have found a vole to eat.

This blackbird is getting a drink of water by eating snow.

Hardy hamster

This Russian hamster is well adapted to life in the cold. Its white coat **camouflages** it. It can also live beneath the snow, eating moss and stores of seeds. The snow traps the animal's body heat, insulating it and so keeping it warm (see pages 20–21).

Cold experiment

COLD FINGER

You need
• Ice cubes
• Bowl

Did you know?

When the female Emperor penguin has laid her eggs, the male stands for 64 days on the Antarctic ice, in temperatures as low as minus 85°F, with the egg resting on his feet. He keeps it warm until it hatches.

1 Half fill a bowl with cold water and put in some ice cubes. Wait 3–4 minutes for the water to cool to 32°F. Put one hand in the water. How long can you keep it there?

2 Dry your cold hand and compare it with the other. Does it look a different color? Does it stay colder or become hotter than your other hand?

Cold makes blood flow in the skin to try to warm it up quickly.

Hearty huskies

Huskies are a special breed of dog that can survive the cold. They are big and strong and have very thick coats. People living in Arctic areas train huskies to pull sleds. A team of dogs is harnessed to each sled. Working together, they can pull heavy loads of people and goods.

Keeping warm

In most parts of the world, the air temperature is cooler than the body temperature of warm-blooded animals. Mammals have fur to keep them warm, birds have feathers, and humans have hair and clothes. This heat-stopping layer is called **insulation**. A still layer of air is one of the best insulators because it conducts very little heat away. Light, fluffy clothes are the best protection from the cold because they trap a layer of insulating air around the body.

Chinchillas live high in the Andes, where it is very cold. They have some of the softest fur of any mammal. Soft fur traps more air, and so is warmer than rough fur.

To keep warm, animals have to eat. Food and oxygen together help to produce the energy that warms their bodies. This missel thrush has found an apple to eat lying in the snow.

Birds can fluff their feathers up and so increase the amount of air trapped around their bodies. The robin (below left) has fluffed its feathers up to keep itself warm.

Did you know?

In water measuring 59°F, people can survive for up to six hours, but at 54.5°F they soon die because they cannot produce enough heat to replace that lost into the water.

These mountaineers are just waking up after a night spent in the Himalayas, where it is extremely cold. Their clothes and sleeping bags are filled with goose down, which is made from the soft fluffy feathers next to a goose's skin. It is very warm and light and so is very useful on such expeditions.

Cold experiment

WARM UP WARM!

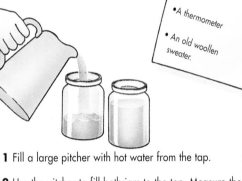

1 Fill a large pitcher with hot water from the tap.

2 Use the pitcher to fill both jars to the top. Measure the temperature of the water with a thermometer before screwing on the lids.

3 Cover one jar with the woollen sweater.

4 Measure the temperature in both jars at regular intervals. Keep a record of your readings. How much longer does the covered jar stay hot?

The sweater provides insulation and so keeps the covered jar warm longer.

Mighty mouse

If you work hard physically, or run fast, you soon find yourself getting warm. Working muscles make heat. Small animals, such as this mouse, run and jump in their search for food. This activity helps them to keep warm.

Hibernation

Some animals hibernate, which means they sleep through winter and wake up in spring. Many cold-blooded animals (see pages 24–25) hibernate because there is no food for them in winter and their bodies just will not work in the cold. Some warm-blooded animals also hibernate. Bats and dormice get fat in the fall before finding a quiet place to sleep. Their body temperature falls and their breathing and heartbeat become slow and faint. If disturbed, hibernating animals can wake themselves up by breathing hard.

Ladybird clusters

Insects are cold-blooded. Many die before winter, but some hibernate. Ladybugs often hibernate in clusters, like these. Often they will hibernate in the same place each year.

Did you know?

Some small mammals hibernate so deeply that they seem dead. You cannot see them breathing and they do not wake up even if you pick them up and uncurl their bodies!

Emerging Toad

Snails and toads, which are cold-blooded, also hibernate. Toads crawl under logs and stones. Their bodies get so cold that they can hardly move. Here a toad has chosen to hide in the same place as some snails. Spring is coming, so the toad is awake and looking out.

Polar bears

Winter in the Arctic is dark and very cold. Male polar bears prowl about hungrily, but females dig a deep cave in the snow. There they give birth to their cubs. When spring arrives, they come out.

Cold-blooded animals

Cold-blooded animals, such as insects, fish, and **reptiles**, cannot control their body temperature. When the weather is hot, they are hot and active. In cold weather, they are cold and sluggish. They do not need to eat a lot to keep warm. But they cannot run fast on cold days, and may be caught by a predator.

All present-day reptiles are cold-blooded, but nobody really knows if the giant dinosaurs that lived on Earth millions of years ago were cold-blooded or not. Some people think they may have been warm-blooded. The two Tyrannosaurus seen in this mock-up picture are fighting over prey and they look pretty hot-blooded about it!

Amphibians, such as this frog, are cold-blooded. They cannot move at speed for very long. A frog can only do four or five long leaps before it becomes tired.

Fish are the same temperature as the water they swim in. They can swim fast for only short periods of time. This archerfish put on a great burst of speed to leap out of the water to catch a fly.

Cold experiment

ANTICS

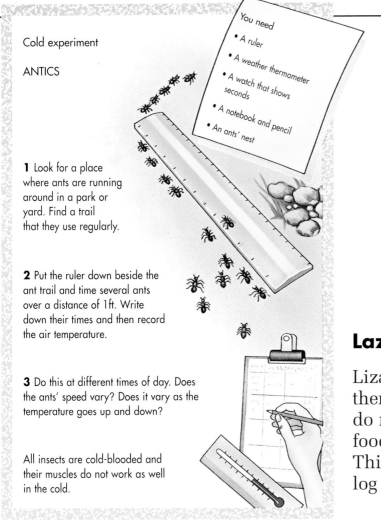

1 Look for a place where ants are running around in a park or yard. Find a trail that they use regularly.

2 Put the ruler down beside the ant trail and time several ants over a distance of 1ft. Write down their times and then record the air temperature.

3 Do this at different times of day. Does the ants' speed vary? Does it vary as the temperature goes up and down?

All insects are cold-blooded and their muscles do not work as well in the cold.

Lazy lizard

Lizards spend hours sunning themselves to warm their bodies. They do not need to eat very much because food is not used to give them warmth. This male agama lizard is resting on a log watching over his territory.

Skinks are smooth shiny lizards with small legs. They slither along rather like a snake. They also gather heat from the sun and can only move fast when their bodies are warm.

Did you know?

One kind of lizard living in the high mountains of South America can absorb the sun's heat so well during the day that it can raise its body temperature to 95°F when the air around measures only 50°F.

25

Cold places

Antarctica, the land around the South Pole, is the coldest place on Earth. The average temperature in one area called "the pole of cold" is minus 72.5°F. However, much colder temperatures occur in the **upper atmosphere** where they can drop to minus 225°F.

In both the Antarctic and the Arctic, the area around the North Pole, the ground never thaws out. A few inches on top may thaw in the summer, but there is always ice underneath. This permanently frozen ground is called **permafrost**. In Arctic areas of Russia the permafrost may be nearly a mile deep. Thousands of years ago, during the Ice Ages, the world was much colder and the Arctic ice cap reached down well into Europe and North America.

Huge hairy elephants called mammoths used to live in Europe and North America during the Ice Ages. The frozen body of a mammoth was found in Arctic Russia in 1860. The people excavating the 10,000-year-old animal tried cooking mammoth steaks to see what they tasted like! This picture shows people looking at the stuffed skin of the mammoth, which was put on public display.

Inuit people have lived in the Arctic for centuries and have learned how to survive there, using snow houses and dog sleds. Much of the Arctic is actually frozen sea. The Antarctic, at the other end of the world, is frozen land. Antarctic temperatures are so cold that the only people living there are scientists who go there to study it.

North and South

These pictures show icebergs in the Arctic (top) and off the coast of Antarctica (below). They look very similar, but the wildlife varies. There are no penguins in the Arctic and no polar bears in the Antarctic.

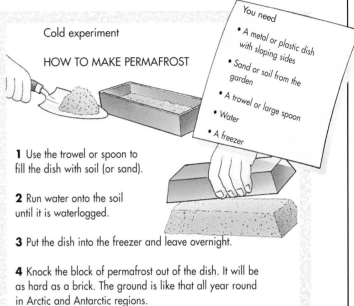

Cold experiment

HOW TO MAKE PERMAFROST

You need
- A metal or plastic dish with sloping sides
- Sand or soil from the garden
- A trowel or large spoon
- Water
- A freezer

1 Use the trowel or spoon to fill the dish with soil (or sand).

2 Run water onto the soil until it is waterlogged.

3 Put the dish into the freezer and leave overnight.

4 Knock the block of permafrost out of the dish. It will be as hard as a brick. The ground is like that all year round in Arctic and Antarctic regions.

Igloo

Arctic snow houses called igloos are made from snow cut into blocks and sealed together with more snow. Igloos are warm inside because the air trapped between the snow crystals makes good insulation. Some light comes through the walls, as you can see here.

Effects of coldness

Making something cold can change it in various ways. If you make metal cold it contracts, or shrinks in size. Cold also slows some things down. That is why plants grow more slowly, and animals move more slowly, in cold conditions. Liquids, such as water, freeze when they get cold enough to reach their freezing point. Extreme cold can kill plants and affect the way bodies work. Frozen body parts can develop **frostbite**. Badly frost-bitten fingers or toes sometimes drop off!

At first, water contracts (shrinks) as it cools down (see the colored water experiment on the opposite page). But if you go on cooling it down below 39°F, it begins to expand (get bigger). This bottle of water has been frozen. Ice has expanded out of the top like an icicle.

Cold chicken

There is frostbite in the darkened tips of this cockerel's comb. Frostbite happens when ice crystals form inside the body cells. The water in the cells expands as it freezes, damaging the cells. If many cells are affected, serious damage is caused. Frostbitten human fingers and toes go hard, cold, white, and bloodless. After thawing, blisters appear on the skin.

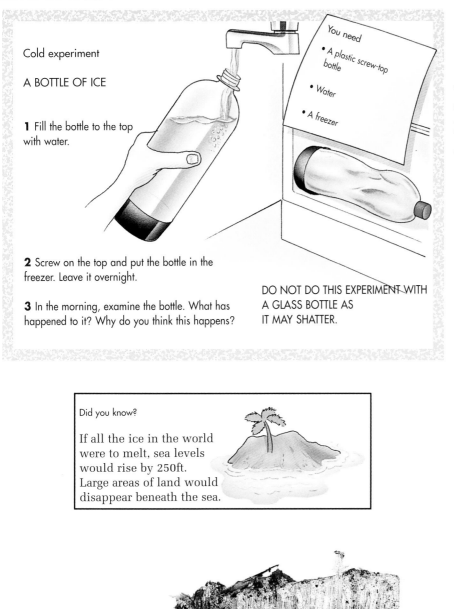

Cold experiment

A BOTTLE OF ICE

You need
- A plastic screw-top bottle
- Water
- A freezer

1 Fill the bottle to the top with water.

2 Screw on the top and put the bottle in the freezer. Leave it overnight.

3 In the morning, examine the bottle. What has happened to it? Why do you think this happens?

DO NOT DO THIS EXPERIMENT WITH A GLASS BOTTLE AS IT MAY SHATTER.

Water contracts (shrinks) a little as it cools, so cold water (with a temperature above 4°C) is more dense than warm water. When cold water is added to warm, the colder water sinks to the bottom.

Cold water (with coloring in it) is about to be added to a tank of warm water.

As the cold water pours in, it sinks quickly to the bottom.

Did you know?

If all the ice in the world were to melt, sea levels would rise by 250ft. Large areas of land would disappear beneath the sea.

When there is a hard frost, the water in the ground freezes. Sometimes water is forced upwards out of the soil to form ice that looks like a honeycomb. You can see some of this frozen ground in the picture below.

Above is a close-up view of some of the honeycomb ice. There are three layers of ice, each formed one night during a spell of cold weather.

The cold water spreads out, forming a cold layer at the bottom of the tank.

Uses of coldness

Today, coldness can be created artificially with freezing equipment, sometimes using special chemicals. This coldness is used in many ways: to transport and store food and medical supplies, to air-condition buildings and aircraft, and to create artificial ice for sport. Freezing probes are used in some surgical operations. There are even fridges on spacecraft to keep equipment cool.

Ouch!

Coldness can help to ease pain. Next time you bump or bruise yourself, try holding a bag of frozen peas on the aching part. But ask permission first as the peas may defrost and need to be eaten soon!

Skating on thin ice

As a skater moves over the ice, the blades on the skates melt the ice a little. This forms a thin layer of water just under the blade, so the skater slides easily. The water refreezes behind the blade.

Ice sports

Because people can travel quickly over ice, many fast and exciting ice sports have been invented. These men are playing ice hockey.

Cold experiment

MAKE YOUR OWN WATER ICE

This recipe makes a simple and delicious dessert.

You also need a pan, lemon squeezer, grater, plastic fridge box, egg beater and a bowl.

You need
- 1 pint (500ml) water
- About 175g (7oz) sugar
- A lemon
- 1 egg white
- A freezer or refrigerator

1 *Ask an adult to help you* while you boil the water and sugar in a pan until the sugar has dissolved. Remove it from the heat.

2 Squeeze the lemon and put the juice into the sugary water. Grate a dessertspoonful of lemon rind into it too.

3 Leave this mixture to cool, then pour it into the plastic box. Put it in a freezer or ice-making part of a refrigerator.

4 After an hour or so, take the box out of the freezer while the lemon ice is still half frozen and mushy. With a beater, beat the egg whites until stiff in a bowl. Fold them into the ice mixture.

5 Put the mixture back to freeze until it is firm.

6 Eat it!

Frozen food

Cold slows down the growth of the **bacteria** that make food go bad. Household fridges store food at around 34° to 45°F. Freezers store food at 10° to minus 10°F. Trucks often transport food packed in "**dry ice**" made from solid carbon dioxide. This is much colder, at minus 110°F.

This lobster is being kept chilled on ice before being served in a restaurant.

Did you know?

The ancient Romans used to eat icecream. They probably made it from snow mixed with honey or fruit.

Cold words

Absolute zero Minus 350°F (Minus 273°C), which is the coldest temperature possible.

Annual Plant that grows for one year only.

Bacteria Microscopic creatures.

Bulb A rounded food store formed by some plants from underground swellings of the leaf bases.

Camouflage Colors or markings that make animals or plants difficult to see in their surroundings.

Condense To turn from a gas into a liquid.

Conduction Movement of heat through something. Heat is conducted from a hot drink through a teaspoon into your fingers.

Convection Movement of heat as a result of rising currents of air or water.

Corm A rounded food store formed by some plants from underground swellings of the stem.

Crystal A solid with a regular geometric shape, formed from regular arrangements of molecules.

Density A measure of the heaviness of a material. Metals are more dense than water, so they sink. Cork is less dense, so it floats.

Dry ice Solid carbon dioxide gas at minus 110°F.

Energy Power or force needed to move something.

Evaporate To change from a liquid or solid into gas.

Freeze To turn from a liquid to a solid.

Frostbite Injury to the body caused by cold.

Hibernate To sleep through the winter.

Insulation Material that slows the loss of heat.

Migrate To move to another lace.

Perennial Plant that lasts for more than two years.

Permafrost Permanently frozen ground.

Prism A block of clear material, usually glass, that bends light rays as they pass through it.

Radiate To travel outwards in waves, as heat energy does from the bars of a glowing electric fire.

Reptiles Cold-blooded, dry-skinned animals with scales, such as snakes and lizards.

Rhizome A root-like underground stem formed by some plants.

Sap Liquid in the stems and leaves of plants.

Upper atmosphere Part of the blanket of gases that surrounds the Earth. The coldest part is about 50 miles above the Earth's surface.

Vibrate To move backward and forward rapidly.

Water vapor Molecules of water moving about in the air in the form of gas.

Index

PICTURE CREDITS
All photographs are by Kim Taylor and Jane Burton except for those supplied by B and C Alexander: 11 *bottom*, 26 *bottom*, 27 *top and bottom*; Bruce Coleman *Robert Burton*: 15 *bottom left*; Eye Ubiquitous: 4 *top*, 9 *bottom*, 10 *left*, 14 *bottom right*, 15 *bottom right*, 30 *bottom left*, 31; Hulton Deutsch: 26 *top*; Zefa: 4 *bottom*, 5 *top*, 10 *top right*, 13 *bottom*, 19, 21 *top right*, 23, 27 *middle*, 30 *bottom right*